Science-Hobby Book of
Rocks and Minerals

A Check-list of the Most Common Minerals, Rocks and Metals Found in the Fifty States:

Alabama: barite, graphite, hematite, muscovite, corundum, coal.

Alaska: gold, copper, silver, chromite, mercury, platinum, antimony, tungsten, asbestos, iron, nickel, marble, jade, lead, bituminous and subbituminous coal.

Arizona: copper, gold, silver, barite, vanadium, uranium, gypsum, turquoise, agate.

Arkansas: garnet, galena, manganese, quartz, rutile, bauxite, diamond.

California: agate, barite, carnelian, cinnabar, galena, quartz, garnet, gold, gypsum, silver, copper, boron, magnesite, uranium, beryl.

Colorado: aquamarine, copper, galena, garnet, gold, orthoclase, pyrite, quartz, topaz, uraninite, silver, molybdenite.

Connecticut: barite, beryl, feldspar, garnet, mica, rutile, topaz, tourmaline, limestone.

Delaware: apatite, beryl, garnet, black tourmaline.

Florida: coral, limestone, phosphate, rutile, ilmenite.

Georgia: asbestos, corundum, gold, granite, hematite, lazulite, marble, quartz, rutile, kaolin.

Hawaii: basalt, bauxite, pumice, coral, titanium oxide.

Idaho: copper, gold, pyrite, quartz, silver, gypsum.

Illinois: calcite, dolomite, fluorite, galena, pyrite, shale.

Indiana: oölitic limestone.

Iowa: galena, gypsum.

Kansas: galena, gypsum, halite, lead, zinc.

Kentucky: calcite, fluorite, gypsum, pyrite.

Louisiana: gypsum, halite, sulphur.

Maine: apatite, beryl, feldspar, fluorite, galena, garnet, mica, pyrite, rose quartz, topaz, green and black tourmaline, zircon.

Maryland: asbestos, chlorite, copper, magnetite, marble, mica, smoky quartz, black tourmaline.

Massachusetts: agate, apatite, beryl, feldspar, garnet, asbestos, graphite, mica, pyrite, rutile, talc, granite, tourmaline.

Michigan: alabaster, amethyst, calcite, copper, gypsum, halite, quartz, silver.

Minnesota: agate, copper, hematite, iron, magnetite, orthoclase.

Mississippi: calcite, limestone, bauxite, bentonite.

Missouri: barite, calcite, chert, fluorite, galena, hematite, limestone, sandstone, sphalerite.

Montana: amethyst, garnet, gold, smoky quartz, sapphire, silver, copper, uranium, sphalerite.

Science-Hobby Book of
Rocks and Minerals

GRAND LEDGE PUBLIC SCHOOL
Greenwood Library

by
MIRIAM GILBERT

ILLUSTRATED BY **WALTER FERGUSON**

BARBARA AMLICK

JOANNE COONS

HERBERT PIERCE

Published by
LERNER PUBLICATIONS COMPANY
Minneapolis, Minnesota

To MY FATHER

who has a heart of "rock" — pure gold

Third Printing 1973

Revised edition copyright © 1968 by Lerner Publications Company
Original copyright © MCMLXI by Hammond Incorporated

International Standard Book Number: 0-8225-0556-8
Library of Congress Catalog Card Number: 68-54179

Manufactured in the United States of America

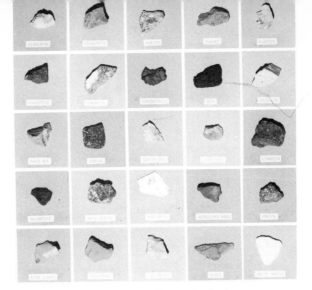

A sample rock and mineral collection

Foreword

What kind of nature enthusiast are you?

Are you the kind who likes to hike through fields and woods, along streams and lakes to find out about nature first hand? Are you the kind who likes to set up exhibits of live things such as fish and reptiles and growing plants, or to make collections of inanimate things such as rocks and shells and pressed flowers? Or are you possibly the kind who prefers to sit quietly at home reading about nature?

To become a real naturalist you need to be all three kinds.

By getting out into nature you'll see how plants grow, how animals live, and find out how plants and animals depend on each other. By bringing home specimens you'll have a chance to study them at leisure and in close detail. And then, reading about them, you will find out the correct names for what you have seen and collected and will learn what other naturalists have discovered about them.

By going about your nature pursuits in this way, you will pick up a science hobby that will give you hours and days of enjoyment for the rest of your life. But not only that: you will learn to use your eyes to *observe* things, your mind to *figure out* things, and your hands to *do* things — three very important parts of the training of a budding scientist.

WILLIAM HILLCOURT

Author of BOY SCOUT HANDBOOK and

FIELD BOOK OF NATURE ACTIVITIES AND CONSERVATION

CONTENTS

AGATE

Starting a Rock
and
Mineral Collection

Man looks up into the sky, reaching for the stars, without realizing the riches and wonders that lie in the ground at his feet. History has left its imprint in rocks and minerals. You can unravel some of the mystery of the ages by starting and studying a rock and mineral collection.

In an elementary sense, the study of rocks and minerals is known as geology. In the scientific sense, geology embraces the study of the earth and its life, as recorded in rocks. It is a science that reaches out into other sciences, as note for example, the definition given in *Webster's Unabridged Dictionary* which states: "Geology utilizes the principles of physics, astronomy, chemistry, mineralogy, zoology, botany, etc." Thus, in its broadest sense, the study of rocks and minerals is the study of the development and progress of man through the ages.

But where to begin? How to begin? Do you need any scientific training or knowledge? Sometimes all you need is a pebble in your shoe. You take it out and something about it strikes you as odd. It may look shiny, it may feel waxy. But something has caught your attention and intrigued you — and you have taken your first step toward becoming a rock hound.

Rocks are all about you; at excavation sites for new houses, at the seashore, in the woods, along mountain trails and across trackless deserts. Start with your own local area first and branch out from there. You may be fortunate and live close to or visit a region that is noted for its unusual rock formations but even a city dump may contain rock treasures, dating back tens of thousands of years. If you live in Vermont near a quarry, or in Pennsylvania near a mine, this may be the place for you to get your first samples. You will be able to buy hard-to-find specimens from various natural science supply houses or, through trading and exchanging, you can build up a varied collection that has no geographical limitations but can be world-wide in scope.

Just where, when, and how the first rocks occurred is difficult to say. Although there have been many theories about the formation of the earth, scientists are still not certain as to its origin. However, they generally agree that some 4½ billion years ago the earth was still in a molten state and as this mass cooled a crust formed and solidified into the "first rocks" of the world. Rocks which have cooled from a molten state are called igneous, which means "fire-formed." The rocky crust of our earth is known as the lithosphere, which means "ball of rock."

Trapped deep within the heart of the earth is searing hot, molten rock, known as magma. This mass of molten rock and metals moves and shifts, sometimes imperceptibly, sometimes violently. Whenever it finds a crack, it escapes in the form of lava, shooting up out of the earth, and we have the phenomenon of a volcano. As the magma changes its position below, the earth's surface adjusts its position above. When there is a sudden shift, an earthquake results. Mountains and lakes have been formed, islands have appeared and vanished, because of a change in the earth's crust. Sometimes magma, as it forces its way upward through weak spots, encounters underground water which is thrust above the surface as geysers. Thus, the earth, and its rocks and the rocks on it and which are a part of it, are in a state of constant flux and change. Nature is a miser. Rocks are formed and re-formed, shaped and re-shaped, changed from one substance into another again and again and again. Nature maintains, however, an orderly and logical plan in the midst of this unceasing change. This orderly progression is evidenced in the formation of rocks and minerals. Atoms make elements, elements form minerals, minerals combine to make rocks.

WHAT ARE THE DIFFERENCES BETWEEN ROCKS AND MINERALS?

The terms, rocks and minerals, are frequently used interchangeably, yet there are major differences.

Stated in the simplest terms: Minerals are elements in chemical combination. Rocks on the other hand, are large masses of minerals. Most rocks consist of two or more minerals mixed together; some rocks are made up only of one mineral. Minerals have definite characteristics of their own; a rock depends on the minerals in it for form, color as well as other specific characteristics.

Scientists have checked, collated and collected nearly 2,000 minerals. Of this number, only about 30 are found in large quantities in rocks, and are called rock-forming minerals. We will discuss slightly more than half of the more important and most common rock-forming minerals.

ROCK CLASSIFICATION

Rocks are divided into three main classes according to their origins. These are — igneous, sedimentary and metamorphic.

If the fire-formed igneous rocks may be called our "first rocks," sedimentary rocks are our second rocks. They are known as sedimentary because they have been formed through the ages by "sediment." Wind, waves, weather and water pounded away unyieldingly, grinding the igneous rocks into smaller and ever smaller bits, until nothing remained but dust and sand — sediment. This sediment was swept along until it settled to the bottoms of rivers, lakes and oceans. Year after year, the relentless process continued. Layer upon layer was formed, the new sediment on the top, crushing and pushing down the bottom layer, until what was fine dirt solidified into a hard rock.

Year followed year, century followed century and through a variety of ways, such as earthquakes, or a decrease in the water level, sedimentary rocks became exposed.

These sedimentary rocks are our first history books — natural picture books — for many specimens have been discovered which contain the impress of plants and the tracks of animals. These fossil pictures have unlocked the secrets of what many extinct animals looked like, and the kind of plants that existed in the distant past. Fossils have been well-preserved in sedimentary rocks because the rocks were in the process of formation during the time these plants and animals lived. Geologists have also been able to estimate the approximate ages of rocks by the fossils found in them.

The third group is the metamorphic rocks. As the first rocks were weighed down by other massive rocks, the pressure, plus heat and water, re-shaped and altered them. These rocks are known as "metamorphic" because as in the metamorphosis of animals, such as the frog, the form has changed from its original condition.

Shishaldin Volcano
Unimak, Aleutian Islands

U.S. Navy Photo

FLINT
A mineral that creates fire

ORGANIZING YOUR ROCK COLLECTION

Just as there is logic and order in nature, there should be a definite plan for your rock collection. At the beginning, you may start out haphazardly gathering together as many and as large a collection of rocks and minerals as you can find. But once you are well underway, you should start thinking about classifying your "finds" along specialized, even scientific, lines. Here are some suggestions for grouping your collection:

GENERAL: The collection should be set up so that minerals are separated from the rocks. A further division would be to divide the rocks into the three major categories: igneous, sedimentary and metamorphic. This type of basic organization should be applied to all your collections, no matter how specialized.

GEOGRAPHICAL (LOCAL): Gather together the various rocks and minerals for which your state is known; see how many varieties you can find within your own neighborhood.

TRAVEL MEMENTOES: Build a rock record of vacation trips by collecting specimens of rocks in the different regions you visit.

PHYSICAL PROPERTIES: The physical properties and characteristics of rocks and minerals can serve as the focal point of your collection. In this grouping, you could have a *cleavage collection,* showing the different kinds of cleavage that occur in minerals; a *fracture collection,* illustrating such fractures as even, uneven, conchoidal, sub-conchoidal, splintery and hackly; a *luster collection,* revealing the various types and degrees of luster; a *crystal collection,* containing examples from the six systems of crystallography.

NATURAL HISTORY: This could contain a grouping of fossils. You could get a good start by buying a beginner's collection from one of the natural science supply houses since a variety of fossil remains is not easily obtained.

Another collection, in the natural history area, could consist of rock slabs or layers (for instance, limestone, flagstone or shale) which carry the imprint of nature in action through the ages, such as ripple marks of tides and tracks of prehistoric animals.

AGRICULTURAL: If you live on a farm, you may be interested in specimens illustrating various rocks broken down into different kinds of soil.

ANTHROPOLOGICAL: Primitive man early realized the value of stone and used it in his daily life. The Paleolithic Age, which is sometimes called the Old Stone Age, began about a million years ago and extended to 8,000 B.C. Objects have been uncovered which show that paleolithic man shaped stone to make axes, spears, knives and other implements. In the Neolithic period, designated as the New Stone Age, man added refinements and learned how to polish stone. Tools made by the Indians in North and South America would make an especially interesting collection. This would encompass a variety of stones since the Indians were adept at chipping and polishing rocks, and also did mining. Arrowheads of flint come to mind first since they are such a familiar item associated with Indian legend and lore, but you could also include samples of catlinite or pipestone from which the Indians fashioned their "peace" pipes and sharp pointed knives of obsidian, found in volcanic areas.

ARTISTIC: Nature has created patterns and designs of her own in rocks which would create an interesting and beautiful collection. An assorted array of marbles in all the many colors, designs and textures, for example, is a fine idea for anyone interested in a specialized collection. Of course, jade which has been known for centuries for its adaptability for carving, is a magnificent stone around which to build a collection in which visual beauty may be more important than the scientific qualities.

HOW TO IDENTIFY MINERALS

As an amateur, you will want to learn to identify as many of the common minerals as you can in order to help you classify your rocks. There are several scientific methods which you can use to guide you in mineral identification. Minerals have certain definite, precise characteristics, or "physical properties," as they are called. Hardness is one of these qualities. Each mineral has a certain degree of hardness, which can be tested. It is not a question of hardness, in the layman's common parlance of firm or solid; basically it is a resistance test. The hardness of a mineral is determined by the way it resists scratching. For scientific purposes, a hardness gauge, known as Mohs scale, is used.

DIAMOND
Nature's hardest substance

HARDNESS: Ten minerals, each representing one degree on the hardness scale, are used to test graduations of hardness, varying from talc, which is the softest, to diamond, which is the hardest.

  1 — Talc
  2 — Gypsum
  3 — Calcite
  4 — Fluorite
  5 — Apatite
  6 — Orthoclase
  7 — Quartz
  8 — Topaz
  9 — Corundum
10 — Diamond

If you have an unknown mineral, which you are testing for hardness, and it scratches calcite but not fluorite, the mineral has a hardness of between 3 and 4. This is the start for narrowing the field and bringing you closer to a more positive identification. As a guide, any mineral will scratch another mineral of a lower number. Two minerals of the same number (hardness) will scratch each other.

If you want to start out on a small basis and yet have some general means of identification, you can use a penny, a knife, and a piece of glass.

According to the varying degrees of hardness, here are the ways in which you can test unidentified minerals for hardness:

  1 — Scratches very easily with fingernail; is greasy to the touch.
  2 — Can be scratched with the fingernail but lacks the greasy "feel."
  3 — Can be scratched with the edge of a penny; too hard to be scratched with the fingernail.
  4 — Easily scratched with knife; cannot be scratched by a penny.
  5 — Knife will barely scratch.
  6 — Scratches ordinary glass easily.

Ward's Natural Science Establishment, Inc.

CALCITE

FLUORITE, cleavage octahedron

Ward's Natural Science Establishment, Inc.

7 — Scratches a knife.

8 — Scratches quartz.

9 — Scratches topaz.

10 — Scratches topaz and corundum. Cannot be scratched by any substance except diamond.

The last three are gem stones and not likely to be encountered by the amateur. You may obtain a set of the hardness minerals from any rock and mineral supply house.

SPECIFIC GRAVITY: The next scientific test that is generally used in mineral identification is that of testing specific gravity. This is the weight of any material in proportion to the weight of an equal volume of water. Some minerals are lighter than water, but others are heavier. Copper, for example, has a specific gravity of 8.9 which means that it is 8.9 times as heavy as an equivalent volume of water. If a mineral weighs six pounds, and the amount of water it displaces weighs three pounds, we say the specific gravity is 2.

CLEAVAGE: This is the way a mineral splits. If it splits with a smooth, flat surface, the mineral is said to have good cleavage. The number of cleavage directions may vary from a single cleavage plane to several. Mica has a single cleavage plane; that is, it splits in only one direction. Feldspar splits in two directions; calcite in three.

FRACTURE: This takes place when a mineral breaks on a line which is not parallel to the cleavage plane of the mineral. The kind of fracture varies. It may be rough and uneven, conchoidal (shell-like), splintery, etc.

STREAK: This is the powder left when a mineral is rubbed against a piece of white, unglazed porcelain. You can use the back of a bathroom tile for your test. Scratch the mineral on the tile. The streak or powder it makes will be a clue to the mineral. Most streak powders are white or varying tones of white. But some minerals leave colored streaks. Pyrite, which is yellow, makes a black mark; hematite leaves a red streak.

COLOR, LUSTER AND TRANSPARENCY: These are additional characteristics which aid in identification. Surprisingly, color itself is not always the best guide. Many minerals are colorless or white, some occur in varying shades, and others owe their color to impurities. Despite these limitations, color can aid in identification if combined with other tests.

Luster is judged by the *manner* in which light is reflected from the surface of a mineral. The descriptive terms used include: vitreous or glassy (quartz), metallic (pyrite), waxy (turquoise), pearly (talc), silky (fibrous calcite), etc.

Transparency is the *quantity* of light transmitted. A mineral is transparent if objects are clearly visible through it. A mineral is opaque if no light passes through it. An intermediate degree of transparency would be a translucent mineral in which light passes through but does not clearly reveal the shape of objects. Color has no influence on transparency. Opaque minerals may be light-colored; transparent ones may be dark.

CRYSTAL SYSTEMS: There are thousands of different crystals, in varying forms and shapes. They have been grouped into six divisions, however, known as crystal systems, based on the length and incline of imaginary lines, called axes, passing through the center of the crystal. These systems are: cubic (isometric), hexagonal, tetragonal, orthorhombic, monoclinic and triclinic.

Crystallography is a complex and exacting science but a brief knowledge of the formation of crystals is important in identifying minerals.

The study of crystals starts back at the beginning when the igneous rocks were first forming out of the molten magma. As the magma cooled, tiny crystals of various minerals began to take shape. Most minerals have a shape, characteristic of their kind. Quartz crystals have six smooth sides, feldspar crystals have four sides.

Given adequate space and time in which to grow, the minerals developed a definite angular form, with smooth faces. If they were so crowded that they couldn't take on their "true" crystal shape, they assumed a "crystalline" structure. Crystals may grow indefinitely by the addition of material from the outside, and gradually the crystals grew larger. Also, the longer it took for the magma to cool, the larger the crystals became. Crystals that develop rapidly are smaller than those that form more slowly. If you see a smooth-grained igneous rock, you will know that it cooled quickly. On the other hand, a coarser-grained igneous rock took longer to cool.

MINERALS

The two most common rock-forming minerals, which can be found in all parts of the world, are feldspar and quartz.

THE FELDSPARS

The name feldspar, meaning "field stone" is applied not to one but a group of minerals. Feldspar is an essential part of such rocks as granite, syenite, basalt and gneiss, to name but a few, and constitutes at least 60% of all igneous rocks.

The feldspars can be divided into two groups based upon their chemical composition. Feldspars containing potassium are sometimes called potash feldspars. Those containing sodium and calcium are known as plagioclase feldspars.

Orthoclase and plagioclase are among the most important feldspars. Orthoclase is the Greek word for "splitting at right angles" and plagioclase is the Greek word for "splitting obliquely," which describes one of the characteristics of this group accurately.

POTASH FELDSPARS

ORTHOCLASE and microcline are two of the common potash feldspars. They are basically alike, except for the fact that they occur in different crystal systems. *Chemical Formula* — $KAlSi_3O_8$; *color* — when pure, colorless; generally white, pink or red, or pale yellow. *Streak* — white; *luster* — glassy or pearly; *cleavage* — good in two directions; *fracture* — uneven; *hardness* — 6; *specific gravity* —2.57; *crystallization* — monoclinic (orthoclase); triclinic (microcline).

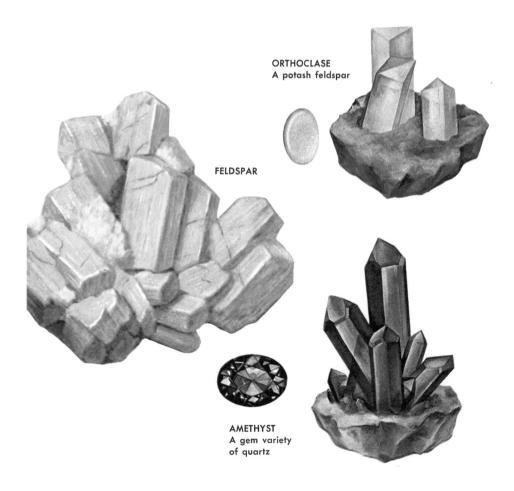

ORTHOCLASE
A potash feldspar

FELDSPAR

AMETHYST
A gem variety
of quartz

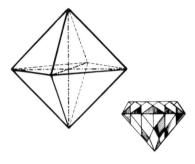

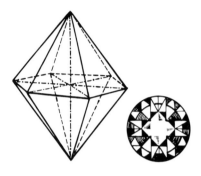

CUBIC SYSTEM
The diamond is an example
of this system

HEXAGONAL SYSTEM
The ruby belongs to this system

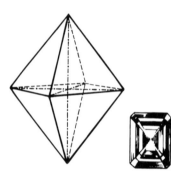

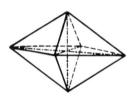

TETRAGONAL SYSTEM
A gem found in this
system is the zircon

ORTHORHOMBIC SYSTEM
The topaz is a valuable gem
occurring in this system

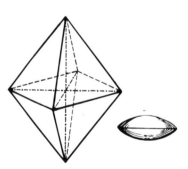

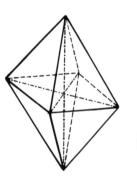

MONOCLINIC SYSTEM
The jade belongs to
this system

TRICLINIC SYSTEM
The moonstone crystallizes
in this system

Fascinating Facts — Many thriving agricultural areas owe their fertile productivity to clay soil which has been released by the gradual weathering of feldspar. In time, through a process of decomposition, the potassium in the rocks crumbles into clay and other vital minerals, such as potash, which stimulates plant life and growth.

Location — Feldspar is found in substantial amounts in many parts of the United States — Virginia and North Carolina in the South; Maine and New Hampshire in New England; Wyoming, South Dakota and Colorado in the West.

Uses — Its clay composition makes feldspar adaptable to the manufacture of porcelain, chinaware, and glass.

ADULARIA is a colorless, transparent variety of orthoclase that is used as a gem. When it is opalescent, it is known as moonstone. A few areas where it is found include: Switzerland, Ceylon, Brazil and Madagascar.

MICROCLINE may be so similar to orthoclase that it is difficult to tell them apart but green microcline, called amazonstone or AMAZONITE, is easy to recognize because of its bluish green color. It is polished and cut into stones for jewelry and ornaments.

Location — Ural Mountains; in the United States — Pennsylvania, Virginia and Colorado.

PLAGIOCLASE OR SODA-LIME FELDSPARS

Minerals in the plagioclase group contain sodium and calcium and are not easily recognized from the potash feldspars except for minor differences in the cleavage. *Chemical Formula* — Sodium and calcium aluminum silicates; albite, which is at one end of the series, contains sodium $NaAlSi_3O_8$; anorthite, which is at the other end of the series contains calcium $CaAl_2Si_2O_8$. Their physical properties are similar to other feldspars. *Color* — white and gray, may also be colorless; *streak* — uncolored; *luster* — vitreous to pearly; *cleavage* — good in two directions; *hardness* — 6; *specific gravity* — 2.62 - 2.76; *crystallization* — triclinic.

In the plagioclase feldspars, the following are interesting:

ALBITE is used by potters because it creates a fine, lustrous coating. Some is cut into moonstones.

LABRADORITE, which comes principally from Labrador, as the name suggests, displays a rainbow fluctuation of colors, ranging from blue and green, to yellow, red, gray or purplish. This striking iridescence has made it popular for jewelry and other adornments.

QUARTZ AND RELATED MINERALS

QUARTZ: *Chemical Formula* — Silicon dioxide SiO_2. This means it is made of silicon (1 atom) and oxygen (2 atoms to 1 molecule). *Color* — Found in a wide range of colors; some transparent, others opaque. It is colorless when pure. The colors are caused by impurities. *Streak* — white; *luster* — vitreous to dull; *cleavage* — rhombohedral; is so indistinct, it is rarely observed; *fracture* — conchoidal; *hardness* — 6.5 - 7; *specific gravity* — 2.5 - 2.8; *crystallization* — hexagonal.

AGATE

Location — Widely distributed throughout the world, including Japan, Switzerland and Canada; large supplies come from Brazil. In the United States, it is found in Arkansas, California, North Carolina and New York.

Uses — in the optical and electronic industries; for ornamental purposes, such as vases and "crystal balls;" has been cut into gems and beads.

ROCK CRYSTAL is the most common of the crystalline varieties. It is pure quartz of water transparency which explains why the Greeks called it "Krystallos" meaning clear ice.

The beauty of quartz is enhanced when it is colored with impurities and the following varieties have been cut into gems:

AMETHYST — the purple or violet variety of crystalline quartz. The rich, royal color is caused by iron or a combination of iron and manganese. It is found in Uruguay, Brazil and Mexico. In the United States, amethysts have been found in the Lake Superior district and in North Carolina, New York, California and Maine.

CITRINE — yellow crystalline quartz, found largely in Brazil. The color is due to iron; is sometimes sold as "Spanish topaz." Most gems marketed as topaz are varieties of quartz, which have been subjected to heat treatment.

ROSE QUARTZ — comes in a rose-pink tone; color is due to manganese; is usually cut cabochon style, which refers to a stone of almost any shape with a flat bottom and an oval top. Location: Japan, Brazil, France. In the United States — Maine, South Dakota, California and Montana.

MILKY QUARTZ — a whitish opaque variety; is seldom cut into gems unless it is gold-bearing. Found in California, Colorado and Alaska.

CHALCEDONY: A transparent or translucent form of quartz, usually light in color, with a waxy luster. It never is crystalline but forms layers or masses. CARNELIAN is a reddish chalcedony, due to ferric oxide. HELIOTROPE, or bloodstone, is a dark green chalcedony with spots of red jasper scattered through it. CHRYSOPRASE is a translucent variety of chalcedony with an apple-green color caused by the presence of nickel oxide.

AGATE: A form of quartz, usually the transparent or translucent chalcedony variety. *Color* — white, gray, yellow, brown and blue; also colorless.

The most familiar agates have bands or stripes of color varying in size, from a quarter of an inch, to some so thin that several thousand are compressed into one inch. These bands are porous and were formed because water containing minerals trickled through rocks, particularly in lava areas, filling in cracks and cavities with rippled layers of silica. Agate is hard and resistant.

Nature has designed a variety of beautiful agates: EYE AGATES have rings of color; CLOUDED AGATES have a hazy appearance, caused by foreign matter; BANDED AGATES have wavy bands of color in irregular widths. The conditions under which each layer was deposited varied; thus the colors vary. MOSS AGATES have a delicate moss-like coating due to dendritic inclusions of manganese dioxide which has worked its way between the layers and spread out in a moss-shaped pattern.

Location — Brazil, Uruguay, South Africa, New South Wales and widely scattered in ancient lava areas. In the United States, agates are found in the Lake Superior area, and in Arizona, California, Oregon and Montana. The Idar-Oberstein area in Germany is noted as an agate cutting and polishing center.

Uses — Commercial agates can be colored artificially because of the porous quality of the bands. Both the natural and commercial varieties are used for jewelry and ornamental purposes. The chemical industry has found that agate is practical for small mortars and pestles, due to its hardness and resistance to acids.

FLINT: A variety of quartz, opaque to translucent, in impure form. *Chemical Formula* — mostly silica, occasionally has a small percentage of calcite and dolomite; *color* — brown, gray, blue-gray, black; *luster* — waxy; *cleavage* — breaks with a conchoidal fracture; *hardness* — 7; *specific gravity* — 2.6; *special characteristics:* it is easily shaped, although it is hard and brittle. *Fascinating Facts:* Flint was used by primitive man in fashioning instruments and tools. In the early stages of civilization, man discovered flint would shoot off sparks to create a fire if it were rubbed against a rock, another piece of flint, or some other hard metallic substance. Flint arrowheads were made by the Indians, and the American pioneers during Colonial times used flintlock guns.

Location — Found throughout the world, but the large chalk deposits of England and France are best-known.

Uses — Not in general use today.

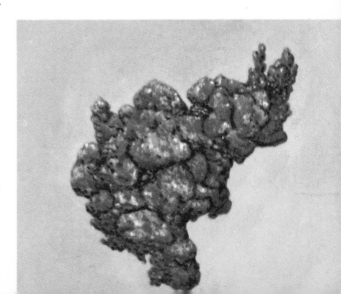

NATIVE COPPER

METALLIC MINERALS

COPPER: This is found both in compound form and in a pure or "native" state. A mineral which occurs naturally and is not combined with other elements is known as a "native" mineral. This is true also of silver and gold, which are often found in solid form. "Native" copper is found in smaller quantities than copper compounds. In the United States, the copper found in the Lake Superior region is often in a nearly pure state. *Chemical Formula* — Most copper minerals are compounds of sulphur and copper. *Cleavage* — none; *color* — reddish-brown; in compound form, it is blue or green; *streak* — metallic; *hardness* — 2.5; *specific gravity* — 8.9; *special characteristics* — easily shaped; a good conductor of electricity; is ductile, which means that it is pliable enough to be drawn out into wires.

Fascinating Facts — Copper has a long history. The Romans and the Egyptians learned how to mix copper with tin to make bronze and many of our museums have examples of this early handiwork. The ancients also combined copper with zinc to make an alloy of brass. North American Indians, who mined copper in the Lake Superior area, appreciated the malleable qualities of the metal and hammered it into many tools.

Location — Bolivia, Australia, Russia. The United States produces about one-quarter of the world's supply, a good part of this coming from the Lake Superior region. It is also mined in Utah, Arizona, Montana, Alaska and New Mexico.

Uses — Among many things, copper is used in making electrical wires and cables and in the manufacture of a good deal of other electrical equipment. It blends readily with a variety of metals and is one of the basic components of such diverse alloys as brass and bronze. It is used in the creation of beautiful jewelry and, in the United States, for penny coins.

Ward's Natural Science Establishment, Inc.

MALACHITE   AZURITE

MALACHITE and AZURITE are carbonates of copper that usually go hand in hand; both are noted for their brilliant colors.

Malachite ($CuCO_3 \cdot Cu(OH)_2$) occurs in an attractive green. Outstanding specimens have been found in Bisbee, Arizona. *Hardness* 3.5 - 4; *specific gravity* 3.9 - 4.03.

Azurite, which is very similar to malachite as can be seen from its chemical composition ($2CuCO_3 \cdot Cu(OH)_2$), comes in a beautiful azure-blue color. *Hardness* 3.5 - 4; *specific gravity* 3.77 - 3.89. Stones for ornaments are cut

A gold dredging machine
in the Yukon

from each of these and make very attractive pieces.

GOLD: Gold, surprisingly, is distributed in many forms and places. It is found in igneous, sedimentary and metamorphic rocks and in minute amounts in all sea water. It is found in grains or nuggets, in thin veins and irregular patches. It is usually mined in conjunction with quartz, copper, silver and other metals. It may be discovered in a lode, which is a deposit in a fissure in the earth's crust, or in a placer deposit, which is simply a place where gold is obtained by washing, and usually consists of sand or gravel, containing particles of gold. Many a prospector, in the early, hectic days of gold mining, panned the metal by hand from these placers. The gold strike that started the mad mass exodus to California was made in placer deposits in the beds of streams carried away from the famous Mother Lode. *Color* — when pure, it is deep yellow; *streak* — golden yellow; *cleavage* — none; *fracture* — rough; *hardness* — 2.5 - 3; *specific gravity* — 19.3. *Special Characteristics:* Malleable, ductile, resistant to rust. Does not tarnish. So soft, it cannot be worked in its pure state but must be alloyed with copper or silver to give it durability. In its alloyed form, gold is considered in terms of carats. This is a mathematical unit of weight, indicating a twenty-fourth part. A fourteen carat (14K) ring would mean that it contained ten parts of alloy to fourteen carats of fine gold.

Location — South Africa, Ontario, Canada, Western Australia and Russia. In the United States — California, Alaska, South Dakota and Utah.

Uses — Gold is the basis of our monetary system. It is also used for jewelry and in gilding decorative objects. Dentists employ it in the familiar form of gold fillings.

SILVER: "Native" silver appears most often in the form of fine twisted wire embedded in rock. Silver also appears as an ore. It is found with copper. Many lead deposits also contain sizable and profitable amounts of silver.

Color — Its characteristic of tarnishing shows up in its "native" form, where it appears with a black or bronze cast. Untarnished, its color is white with metallic overtones. *Hardness* — 2.5 - 3; *specific gravity* — 10.5.

Location — In both its pure and ore state, silver is found heavily concentrated in the western part of the United States; in Arizona, Colorado, Utah, Idaho, and the "Silver State" itself — Nevada. Elsewhere, Mexico and Peru are leading silver producers.

Uses — Like gold, it is used for monetary exchange. It is fashioned into jewelry and tableware. It is employed widely in the photographic industry, as well as being used for specialized purposes by doctors and dentists.

Fascinating Facts — The derivation of the word "sterling" in connection with silver is interesting. It seems that in the 13th century, English coins had little silver, whereas coins minted in northern Germany contained a fairly large proportion of silver. These German coins were known as Easterlings and, with the passage of time, the word became altered to "sterling" and, since then, it has always denoted high-quality silver.

SPHALERITE: Another interesting metallic mineral is Sphalerite (zinc sulfide, ZnS), which is the most valuable ore of zinc. One of the recognizable features is its perfect dodecahedral cleavage. It is one of the metallic minerals that you are most likely to find since it is fairly common. Good sources are found in Missouri, Kansas, Oklahoma, Colorado, Montana, Wisconsin and Idaho. *Hardness* — 3.5 - 4; *specific gravity* — about 4; *color* — usually yellow to yellowish brown; pure specimens are clear; *luster* — resinous.

HEMATITE (Red Iron Ore): To understand the value of the mineral hematite, one must first realize that iron has to be taken out of ore, and hematite is the iron ore from which most of the world's iron and steel is made. Iron is not found in a "pure" state, except in limited amounts on Disco Island, Greenland; and except for this infinitesimal amount, iron has to be extracted from ore. In its pure form, we would recognize the silver-gray color of iron. However, iron which comes from common hematite looks quite different. *Chemical Formula* — Fe_2O_3 — a compound of oxygen and iron; *color* — red; *streak* — blood-red. The name hematite comes from the Greek, meaning "blood-like"; *luster* — none; *hardness* — 5.5 - 6.5; *specific gravity* — 5.3; *noncrystalline*.

Other varieties of hematite are:

RED OCHER — When hematite is mixed with a high percentage of clay, it gets an earthy quality and is called red ocher. In powdered form, red ocher is used in pigment and rouge and was used by the Indians for war paint.

MICACEOUS HEMATITE consists of thin, tiny flakes, almost translucent, and very similar to mica flakes.

Location — Ontario, Canada. In the United States — Minnesota, Michigan and Wisconsin.

Uses — Industrial, household and many other articles, far too innumerable to mention, are made out of iron. From ships to clips; from trains to planes — the world we live in, the world we move in, depends upon products of iron and steel.

PYRITE: Pyrite (iron disulfide, FeS_2) gets its name from the Greek word which means fire. Because of its metallic luster and occasional scattering of copper and gold, it has fooled enough budding mineralogists and prospectors to become known as "fool's gold." It is made up of more than fifty percent sulphur and is the most common mineral found in veins with metallic sulfides. *Hardness* — 6; *specific gravity* 5; *streak* — greenish black.

BERYL

A mineral needed for atomic research

Emerald

Gem varieties of the beryl

Aquamarine

TOURMALINE
Gems found in various colors

TOPAZ

Sapphire

Ruby

CORUNDUM

Star Sapphire

GARNET

URANINITE: Uraninite might be called a modern mineral, perhaps miracle, since it was one of the essential components of the atomic bomb. However, besides being valuable as a source of uranium, it also yields radium. It may help to explain why radium is so expensive if you realize that about 750 tons of ore must be mined in order to obtain the infinitesimal amount of 1 gram of radium.

Uraninite has other unusual characteristics. It is an amazingly heavy metal. Its *specific gravity* is 9 - 9.7; *hardness* 5.5. It is pitchlike, or greasy, in *luster* which accounts for its popular designation as pitchblende. It is composed mainly of UO_2 and UO_3, plus fragmentary amounts of radium, thorium and other elements. Uraninite has been found with pegmatites in Colorado, the New England area, also in North Carolina and Texas.

SOME MINERALS VALUED AS GEMS

When is a mineral a gem? Broadly classified, all minerals and stones that are used for jewelry may be called gems. But more specifically, the following qualities make the difference: beauty and evenness of color; sufficient hardness so that it can be polished; durability; rarity; internal flawlessness as far as possible and, occasionally, transparency and fashion whims.

BERYL: *Chemical Formula* — a beryllium-aluminum silicate; usual formula is $(Be_3Al_2(SiO_3)_6)$; sometimes a portion of the beryllium is replaced by another element. *Color* — Common beryl is light green and white; also a colorless variety is known as goshenite. Color is the guide in the gem species. EMERALD — vivid green; GOLDEN BERYL — yellow; AQUAMARINE — greenish-blue; MORGANITE — pink; *streak* — white; *luster* — vitreous; crystallizes in the hexagonal system; *cleavage* — poor; *fracture* — uneven; *hardness* — 7.5 - 8; *specific gravity* — 2.6 - 2.8.

Fascinating Facts — For many years, the emerald has been ranked as the most costly of all gems.

Location — Common beryl is found in India; in the United States, it is one of the minerals found in the New England area, being mined in Massachusetts,

New Hampshire, Maine, and Connecticut. It also occurs in North Carolina and South Dakota. Beryl of gem quality, such as golden beryl and aquamarine, has also been found in Connecticut. The world supply of emeralds, however, is obtained, for the most part, from Russia.

Uses — Common beryl is combined with copper to make alloys, which are manufactured into many important tools for industrial purposes. It is also used for atomic research.

TOPAZ: *Chemical Formula* $((AlF)_2SiO_4)$ is a valuable gem stone found in pegmatites and granites. *Colors* range from light yellow to brown with some varieties of pink and blue. *Hardness* 8; *specific gravity* 3.4 - 3.6.

TOURMALINE: This is a complex silicate containing boron and aluminum. The *color* is commonly black, although there are red, green, brown and blue varieties. *Hardness* 7.5; *specific gravity* 3.

CORUNDUM: An aluminum mineral known especially for its hardness. *Chemical Formula* (Al_2O_3); *Color* — varieties occur in varying shades of gray, brown and black. The color is due to foreign matter such as iron, chromium, titanium, soda, etc. Gem varieties are: RUBY — red. Rubies with a clear, deep, even color are the rarest of all gems and are treasured more highly than diamonds of equal size. The ruby ranks next after the emerald as a precious gem. SAPPHIRE — blue or pink, ORIENTAL TOPAZ — yellow, ORIENTAL EMERALD — green, ORIENTAL AMETHYST — purple, ORIENTAL WHITE SAPPHIRE — colorless. *Cleavage* — no real cleavage. It often shows parting on the basal plane, which is considered pseudocleavage. *Hardness* — 9; *specific gravity* — 3.9 - 4.15; *crystallization* — hexagonal system.

Fascinating Facts — Star gems, frequently found in the sapphire group and less often among the rubies, are a type of corundum which displays a six-rayed star when cut with a convex surface, or as lapidaries say, when cut "en cabochon." This is the Star Sapphire or Star Ruby so greatly prized.

GARNET: A group of common minerals usually thought of as gems only; found in many colors, but most popularly known for the red garnet variety. They all crystallize in the cubic (isometric) system but vary somewhat in composition. The following are interesting.

GROSSULARITE — *Chemical Formula* — $Ca_3Al_2(SiO_4)_3$ — composed of calcium and aluminum in the form of a silicate; *color* — pink, green, white, gray. A brown variety known as cinnamon-stone comes from Ceylon. *Streak* — light in color; *luster* — resinous to vitreous; *fracture* — conchoidal; *hardness* — 6.5 - 7; *specific gravity* — 3.4 - 4.3.

Location — Transvaal, South Africa. In the United States — Oregon.

ALMANDITE — *Chemical Formula* — $Fe_3Al_2(SiO_4)_3$ — a silicate of iron and aluminum. *Color* — deep red, to violet-red or black. It is the most common variety.

Location — The common garnets are found in the Adirondack Mountains of New York, New Hampshire and North Carolina. The gem variety is found in India, Australia, Ceylon, Uruguay, Brazil. In the United States garnets are found in Colorado.

PYROPE — *Chemical Formula* — $Mg_3Al_2(SiO_4)_3$ — a silicate of magnesium and aluminum; *color* — This is the "precious garnet," which is valued for its dark wine red color; *luster* — resinous to vitreous; *hardness* — 7 - 7.5; *specific gravity* — 3.7 - 3.8; *location* — South Africa. In the United States — Arizona, Colorado, New Mexico and Kentucky.

ANDRADITE — *Chemical Formula* — $Ca_3Fe_2(SiO_4)_3$ — a silicate of calcium and iron; *color* — varies. Emerald-green shade, caused by chromium, is known as Uvarovite, or sometimes "Uralian emerald," since it is found in the Ural Mountains in Russia. Grass-green color is called peridot. Yellow shade is called topazolite because it looks somewhat like the yellow topaz. In opaque black, it is known as melanite. Andradite has a higher dispersion than that of the diamond and when cut expertly for jewelry, it has a remarkable brilliancy.

SOME NONMETALLIC MINERALS

CALCITE (calcium carbonate, $CaCO_3$): This is a name given to a wide variety of minerals, all of which have perfect rhombohedral cleavage. It is the main rock-forming mineral in limestone. An interesting way to test for calcite is to apply a drop of hydrochloric acid to your specimen. If little bubbles of carbon dioxide spring up, you can be reasonably certain that some calcite is present. *Hardness* 3; *specific gravity* — 2.72; *luster* — vitreous; *color* — usually white or colorless, sometimes gray, red, yellow, green or blue.

FLUORITE (calcium fluoride, CaF_2): Fluorite is known as the beauty among the minerals. It has perfect octahedral cleavage and occurs in well-defined crystals in hues as varied as a rainbow. Outstanding examples have been found in England. In the United States, the best deposits occur in the southern part of Illinois. Less important deposits are found in Colorado, New Mexico and New York. *Hardness* — 4; *specific gravity* — 3.2.

APATITE $((CaF)Ca_4(PO_4)_3)$: This is easily confused with other minerals because it is found in a variety of colors. *Hardness* — 5; *specific gravity* — 3.2; *streak* — white. It is widely distributed throughout the world.

GRAPHITE: This mineral is composed of only one element — pure carbon — just like the diamond. Then why isn't graphite a precious jewel? As you may recall, there are several important characteristics that determine the

GRAPHITE

MUSCOVITE
A variety of Mica

ASBESTOS
A fibrous variety
of Serpentine

validity and value of a mineral as a jewel, and graphite lacks most of these desirable qualities.

Graphite is soft, having a *hardness* of only 1 - 2; *specific gravity* 2. It is an unattractive gray-black *color;* has a dull *luster* and is greasy to the touch. To add to all of these shortcomings, it *crystallizes* imperfectly. *Special Characteristics* — It is found in varied forms, as grains, flakes and imperfect six-sided plates and scales. The scales have perfect cleavage parallel to their surface, which means that they can be separated into thinner leaves. The best deposits for commercial use have been found in metamorphic rocks, but graphite has also been found in sedimentary and igneous rocks, as well as in meteorites! Marble, schist, granite and gneiss are a few of the rocks in which it sometimes occurs in irregular masses.

Location — Areas with sizable quantities include: Ceylon, Mexico, Madagascar, and Germany. In the United States — the New England area, in addition to Alabama, Montana, New Mexico, California and Colorado.

Uses — In practical application, the defects have been turned to advantages. The blackening quality of graphite makes it perfect for use as the lead in pencils. In purified, powdered form, it is widely used as a dry lubricant for high speed machinery. Since it is resistant to heat, it is often used in crucibles and furnace linings for foundaries and for stove polish. It is also an excellent conductor of electricity.

ASBESTOS (its Greek root word means incombustible): Asbestos comes from the fibrous variety of SERPENTINE ($Mg_3Si_2O_5(OH)_4$) called *chrysotile*. *Color* — the fibrous form occurs in yellowish brown to light brown shadings, tapering off into white; *streak* — white; *luster* — waxy or silky; *fracture* — conchoidal or splintery; *hardness* — 2.5 - 3; *special characteristics* — Chrysotile will not burn. It does not conduct heat except at unusually high temperatures. It is a pliable mineral with cotton-like fibers which can be separated as threads and woven into cloth.

Location — Serpentine asbestos is found in South Africa, Quebec and Rhodesia. In the United States — Vermont.

MICA: A group of minerals containing silicon, all varieties having one perfect *cleavage*. The most important mica is:

MUSCOVITE, white mica, usually *transparent* and the variety used on a large scale commercially. The name grew out of its use as window glass by the Russians or "Muscovites" in former years. *Chemical Formula* — contains silicon, oxygen, aluminum, potassium and hydrogen, $KAl_3Si_3O_{10}$ $(OH)_2$; *color* — besides white, it comes in green, brown; also colorless; *streak* — white; *luster* — glassy; *cleavage* — very good in one direction, parallel to base of crystal; *hardness* — 2 - 2.5; *specific gravity* — 2.7 - 3; *special characteristics* — When hit, mica splits along parallel lines into flat sheets which have amazing resiliency.

Location — India, the United States — especially North Carolina, Virginia, New Hampshire, Connecticut, Idaho and South Dakota.

Uses — Formerly muscovite was used as isinglass windows in stove doors. Its excellent insulating qualities were soon recognized and today it is widely applied in the electrical and electronics industry. Besides its value in "heavy" industry, it has lighter, brighter uses. It is broken up into fine particles for movie "snow" and is used as greeting card and Christmas decorations.

SULPHUR: Mention this mineral, and anyone familiar with it will hold his nose. When melted, sulphur has a distinctively unpleasant odor, commonly characterized as "rotten eggs." *Cleavage* — imperfect; *color* — usually yellow; also found in green, brown or red; *hardness* — 1.25 - 2.25; *specific gravity* — 1.9 - 2.1; *special characteristics* — It is brittle, tasteless, burns with a blue flame and is a poor conductor of heat. It is found in a pure state where there are volcanoes. Also, occurs as transparent or translucent crystals, generally pyramid-shaped, and in the crystallized state it is found in areas which contain deposits of limestone, gypsum and rock salt.

Location — Spain, Mexico, Japan and Italy. In the United States — Louisiana and Texas. In these areas, sulphur beds, some as much as 125 feet thick, and salt domes are frequently found in the same radius.

Uses — Widely used chemically, medically and industrially since it combines readily with other substances to form sulphur compounds, such as sulphuric acids. Its wide varieties of use are indicated by the fact that it is one of the ingredients used in making gunpowder, and is just as powerful, peacefully, as an insecticide and a fertilizer.

A granite quarry at Elberton, Ga.

TALC: *Chemical Formula* — $H_2Mg_3(SiO_3)_4$ — a hydrated magnesium silicate; *color* — green, gray or yellow; *streak* — white; *luster* — pearly to greasy; *cleavage* — perfect in one direction, which means that it splits into thin, flexible flakes. They bend easily but lack the ability to revert to their original position as mica flakes do. *Hardness* — 1. One of the softest minerals; *special characteristics* — Found in two forms: in flat, smooth layers and in compact masses, known as soapstones, or steatite. It has a peculiar soapy feeling to the touch and is transparent to opaque.

Location — Ontario, Canada. In the United States — Vermont, North Carolina and New York.

Use — This is determined by the form in which it is sold: either powdered or in slabs. Manufacturers of heating appliances and furnaces find talc, in slabs, conducts heat slowly and gives good service as linings. The cosmetic industry uses the powdered form for dusting powder; paper manufacturers use it as a filler.

THREE INTERESTING VARIETIES OF IGNEOUS ROCKS

GRANITE: Granite forms the "heart" of many of our mountains in the West, including large parts of the Rockies. This strong rock, noted for its durability, began as magma. The melted rock cooled slowly underground and did not rise to the earth's surface. The rate of cooling and the kind and percentage of minerals, including silica, alumina, potash and soda varied, and so diverse species and colors of granite came into being. In time, massive

MOUNT RUSHMORE
NATIONAL MEMORIAL
Where the faces of four presidents
are carved into solid granite

violent eruptions forced the granite close to the surface of the earth. *Chemical Formula* — contains two basic minerals: quartz and feldspar, with a smattering of other minerals; *color* — comes in a wide miscellany of colors. By and large, feldspar is the coloring agent. Most granite is usually gray or pink, but impurities in the feldspar produce yellow and green varieties. A brownish red granite is caused by the presence of iron. *Specific gravity* — 2.61 - 2.75.

Fascinating Facts — Granite is a rock known and used throughout the centuries in public buildings. The tomb of General Ulysses S. Grant, in New York City, is made of granite. The famous obelisk, Cleopatra's Needle, was made of granite centuries ago by the Egyptians.

Location — Eastern Canada; the United States, especially the New England states, Minnesota, Wisconsin, California and Georgia.

PEGMATITE: This is an example of a coarse-grained granite whose tremendous size and unique dike formation, among other characteristics, make it worthy of special mention. It occurs in huge crystals because during its developmental process, it cooled slowly. It is also found in dikes. These upright walls of igneous rock were created by magma, violently funneled into a narrow opening. The dikes show a multiplicity of size and structure. One area may show a predominance of quartz; and the same dike, at another point, may have a high proportion of a completely different mineral.

Location — Pegmatites are scattered world-wide.

Use — Pegmatites contain a variety of valuable minerals which range from mica, which we already know is signficant in the electrical industry, to uraninite, the radium producing mineral. It may also be a depository for apatite, beryl, and feldspars, to name but a few others.

BASALT: Volcanic in source, erupted originally in a molten state, before crystallization. Basalt carries identifying traces of its volcanic origin since most basalts show flow structure, bubble holes, steam tubes and other marks left by lava flows. *Chemical Formula* — all basalts contain a great deal of lime, magnesium and iron. *Color* — dark gray, green, purplish, black; *specific gravity* — 2.9 - 3.1.

Special Characteristics — On cooling, lava may turn into basalt, which breaks into four to six-sided columns, with flat sides. Examples of this are the Giant's Causeway in Ireland; the cliffs along the Columbia River in the state of Washington; the Palisades along the Hudson River in New Jersey.

Location — India, the Deccan Plateau where almost 200,000 square miles have been covered with thousands of feet of lava, most of which is basalt. In the United States, particularly in the states of Idaho, Washington and Hawaii.

Use — is crushed and used to surface roads.

OBSIDIAN: Obsidian is volcanic glass. *Chemical Formula* — about two-thirds feldspar and one-third quartz, which makes obsidian very similar in composition to granite. *Color* — usually black; but red, gray, and brown may be found; *fracture* — conchoidal; *hardness* — 5 - 5.5; *specific gravity* — 2.3 - 2.7.

Fascinating Facts — In ancient times, Obsidius, who is called the "godfather of obsidian," introduced this rock to Rome from Ethiopia. It was used for mirrors and fashioned into knives, spearheads and chisels.

Location — in the western part of the United States; Yellowstone National Park contains Obsidian Cliff.

BASALT

OBSIDIAN

SOME SEDIMENTARY ROCKS

SANDSTONE: *Chemical Formula* — sandstone consists of grains of quartz (usually) bound together by some mineral or minerals, such as silica, lime or iron. The grains vary in size. When a piece of sandstone breaks, the grains of sand appear clearly on the split surface. *Color* — white to gray, yellow, buff, brown, red or green. The color is determined by the color of the grains and the cementing mineral agent.

Special Characteristics — All sandstones are porous. Sometimes as much as 25 to 30 per cent of the rock may consist of pores if there is little mineral "binder."

Location — world-wide distribution.

Use — Since sandstone can be quarried in blocks or slabs, it can be easily shaped for buildings. Several well-known European churches are made of sandstone, and in the United States, sandstone built houses, known as "brownstones," enjoyed a vogue for some time in various Eastern cities.

Some interesting varieties of sandstone are:

MICACEOUS SANDSTONE: This sandstone has a preponderance of white mica flakes, giving it a silver coloration when it is split.

FLAGSTONE: Flagstone is another plastic rock which contains mica, plus quartz, feldspar and some clay, and on which animal, weather and water impressions have been found. Flagstone breaks into flat beds and can be quarried in large slabs, a quality which made it popular for sidewalks and floors. Today, it is still used in garden walks and paths.

A narrow gorge cut in sandstone in ancient Edom

Jordan Tourist Attache, N.Y.

AEOLIAN SANDSTONE: This shows evidence of having originally been sand dunes that were buried under the sea. The multi-colored Grand Canyon, in Arizona, through which the driving might of the Colorado River has eaten away layer after layer of rock, is an example of Aeolian sandstone.

SHALE: *Chemical Formula* — Clay, mud and silt are the main ingredients of shale. With such a mixture, it is easy to understand why some types of shale are soft; others, however, have a high percentage of silica and are very hard. *Color* — usually gray; also comes in black, green, brick red, brown, purplish and buff.
Fascinating Facts — Shale has changed little since it was first deposited in the ocean. This is why it is one of the finest sources for fossilized imprints of prehistoric life.
Location — found in almost every part of the world.
Use — Soft shales are used as clay in brick or tile making. Other shales are mixed with limestone for cement. Oil shale contains a high proportion of bituminous material from which oil, tar and ammonia are obtained.

GYPSUM: Gypsum is found as a rock-forming mineral and as a sedimentary rock.
ROCK: May contain the mineral gypsum only, or is found combined with clay, iron oxides, marl and bitumen. *Color* — red, brown, yellow, light gray.
MINERAL: *Chemical Formula* — $CaSO_4 \cdot 2H_2O$ — a hydrous calcium sulphate; *color* — white, buff, pink; *streak* — white; *luster* — glassy, pearly or dull; *hardness* — 1.5 - 2; *specific gravity* — 2.2 - 2.4; *crystallization* — monoclinic.
Fascinating Facts — Gypsum most commonly occurs as massive sedimentary rock. It is believed that the gypsum is formed as a result of the evaporation of mineralized water. The plaster quality of gypsum is due to an interaction of forces. Heat forces water out of gypsum; when water is added, the plaster surprisingly solidifies once more into gypsum.
Location — Canada, France, England, Germany and the United States — New York, Virginia, Ohio, Iowa, Alabama, Arkansas and Oklahoma, which has large deposits and has been nicknamed the "Gypsum State." An interesting configuration of dunes of GYPSUM SAND, which forms in dry, desert lakes, is found at the White Sands National Monument in New Mexico.
Use — In the building industry, it is used for plasterboard, wallboard, and paint.

ALABASTER is a white or lightly tinted variety of gypsum which is carved into statues, vases and other ornamental figures. Coarse alabaster, known as "plaster stone" is used to make plaster of Paris. Gypsum was early quarried near Paris, France, hence the derivation of the name plaster of Paris.

ROCK SALT: *Chemical Formula* — In rock form, it is composed of common salt, called halite by mineralogists and known chemically as sodium chloride (NaC1). *Hardness* — 2.5; *specific gravity* — 2.6.

Miners gouge out valuable rock salt in Louisiana

As a mineral, salt is found in both a solid and solution state. The liquid form is called brine. *Color* — Although you may think of salt as being white, it comes in varying colors, due to iron oxides which make it red or yellowish, the presence of carbon which darkens it to black and clay which gives it a gray cast.

Fascinating Facts — The Great Salt Lake in Utah and the Dead Sea in Israel are two famous examples of inland lakes containing water saltier than ocean water. The explanation is this: As streams and rivers flow along they dissolve the salt that lies in the soil and rocks, sweeping it off to large bodies of water. In time fresh water evaporates and salt solutions remain that become heavily concentrated. In the case of the two lakes mentioned, the salt-bearing water became trapped with no outlet to the ocean. As it evaporated, the salt content became higher and higher.

An odd formation are the salt domes, found in Louisana and Texas in the United States and in Mexico, Germany and several other European countries. They are underground ridges of salt, usually circular, capped by layers of gypsum, limestone or other rock. The salt ridges seem to have been caused by shifts and upheavals in the earth, which smashed through the surrounding rock and strata for several thousand feet and forced the salt into its dome shape.

Salt lies underground almost everywhere in the world. Sometimes the salt occurs so close to ground level, it becomes exposed, and these clusters that cut through the ground are called salt licks. Wild animals are often found gathered at these salt licks.

Gypsum sand dunes

Limestone formation in
Carlsbad Caverns

Red Rocks Amphitheater
in Denver, Colorado
hewn into red sandstone

Location — The United States produces more salt than any other country. *Use* — Aside from the familiar use as seasoning, salt is the basis for many compounds. Chemically, industrially, agriculturally, and medically, it is employed in thousands of diversified ways.

LIMESTONE: *Chemical Formula* — Any rock that contains more than 50 per cent of calcium carbonate, generally in the form of calcite, is designated as limestone. *Color* — white or cream colored when pure; usually darkened gray to black by carbon or tinted buff, yellow, red or brown by iron oxides; *hardness* — 3, when it consists chiefly of calcium carbonate; slightly harder when it is mixed with impurities.

TUFA: Tufa is a porous limestone prevalent in hot springs areas whose waters contain a high degree of calcium carbonate in solution. When the pressure which propelled the water to the surface is eased, the water itself dries up, cools and loses carbon dioxide. This causes calcium carbonate to settle and it forms a crust, which in time builds up into a mound or terrace. In the United States the best-known tufa deposits are at Mammoth Hot Springs in Yellowstone National Park.

TRAVERTINE a hard, compact, banded variety of tufa is also found in large deposits near Mammoth Hot Springs. States where travertine is quarried include: Montana, Florida and Colorado. Travertine takes a splendid polish and its pretty range of colors accounts for its use for walls and interior decorations in many public buildings.

COQUINA: This is an interesting example of limestone produced by animal life. Some species of animals, such as oysters, clams, snails, corals and sea urchins, absorb calcium carbonate from the water and use it to make their shell and bones. When the animals die, the shell and bones are pummeled and crumbled by waves into shell and coral sand. Coquina is a brittle, light-colored limestone formed of these finely smashed shells, bound together with calcite. This kind is found on the Florida coast.

CHALK: A soft limestone made up of the tiny shells of one-celled animals, called *Foraminifera. Color* — usually white, but iron oxide, carbon and other minerals may tint it buff, light gray or flesh.

Location — England and France, among other countries. In the United States, Kansas and Texas.

Use — It is used for such common purposes as writing chalk, as polish for glass, in tooth powder, and in paint.

OÖLITIC LIMESTONE: generally called oölite, consists of round grains of calcite which look like fish eggs. This explains the rock's name which means "eggstone," in Greek.

PISOLITE: basically similar to oölite, contains grains about the size and shape of peas, which is why it is popularly known as "peastone."

STALAGMITES AND STALACTITES: Erosion, in various ways, attacks

Coal strip mine
West Lebanon, Pa.

Canadian National Railways

Standard Oil Co. (N.J.)

Elgin coal mine
Drumheller, Br. Columbia

large limestone beds and eventually creates limestone caves. In these caves water which trickles down from the ceiling, drop by drop, builds up layers of calcite. Stalactite is the name applied to these stone fingers of icicle-like formations that hang suspended from the cave roof; stalagmite is the formation that is built up, by accretion, from the floor. Sometimes the two combine and coalesce into a single pillar from floor to roof.

COAL AND PEAT

COAL traces its beginnings back to plant life. Many eons ago, wild vegetation flourished in huge swamps. When the plants died, they dropped into the water. In their watery graves, the decomposing of the plants slowed down. Bacteria feeding on the dead leaves removed oxygen, which increased the amount of carbon that remained in the plants. As layer upon layer of dead, decaying plants piled on top of each other, the new layers forced water out of those below — and coal began to take shape. Thus, through this cycle, plants are converted into rocks of the coal series.

PEAT is the earliest stage in this series. It gets its start in swamps, bogs and marshes, primarily from plants of a low order. Peat exists in a transitional form and shows two stages: the upper part of a peat bed consists of a yellow or dull brown, spongy rock, made up mostly of decayed plant material. Below lies a firm brown or black clay-like mass, in which the stems, leaves, and other plant parts are in a state of near-total disintegration. Since this bottom layer consists largely of water, peat must be thoroughly dried before it is used.

Location — Occurs in many parts of the world. The Everglades swamplands in Florida are a large peat bog area in the United States.

Use — In Ireland and several other European countries, peat is a fuel substitute. In the United States, it is utilized more for fertilizing.

BITUMINOUS COAL is popularly referred to as "soft coal." It is the most valuable and abundant grade of coal. *Chemical Formula* — carbon (60 to 85 per cent), volatile matter (15 to 40 per cent) and ashes. *Color* — grayish black to deep black in color and visibly banded; *hardness* — 1 - 2.

Fascinating Facts — The layers in bituminous coal disclose "biographical" details about its former life. The layers are actually flattened and compressed tree trunks. The soft parts of the tree disintegrated. The woody section held firm, and gradually became filled with compounds formed by the decay of the soft parts of the wood. Eventually these compounds were reduced to carbon, which is black and shiny, and thus many pieces of bituminous coal have these distinctive glistening black bands.

Location — There are large coal fields in Canada, Europe, Asia, Africa and Australia. In the United States, bituminous coal beds are centered in an area west of the Appalachian Mountains, extending from Ohio and Pennsylvania and reaching as far south as Alabama.

Use — It is widely used as a fuel for homes as well as for industrial heating purposes. It is especially valuable in steel processing, in the form of coke and subsidiary coke derivatives.

ANTHRACITE is the next progression in the coal series. Soft coal that has been tightly compressed becomes metamorphosed into anthracite or "hard coal."

In mountainous areas, such as the Appalachians, the weight of mountains was sometimes shifted over a soft-coal bed and bore down heavily; in this way, water and gas were forced out gradually, and a high concentration of carbon remained. By this process, anthracite was produced — a hard, steely or black colored, brittle rock, with the lowest amount of water and the highest carbon content, ranging from 86 to as much as 99 per cent.

Although anthracite takes longer to burn than soft coal, it creates far less smoke. Consequently it is desirable for home use and is preferentially recommended for cities which have smoke control regulations. Unfortunately, anthracite is available only in limited supply in contrast to bituminous and other coal. In the United States the largest anthracite deposits are in Pennsylvania. Huge deposits are also found in China and Russia; and those in Indochina and the Union of South Africa equal those of Pennsylvania in importance and size.

ANTHRACITE

SOAPSTONE

GNEISS

EXAMPLES OF A FEW METAMORPHIC ROCKS

As you have already found out, metamorphic rock is altered in form and sometimes in its mineral make-up by searing hot magmas, intense pressure and agitated revolutions below surface, or the chemical penetration of liquids and gases.

GNEISS is a metamorphic rock, consisting of the same mineral composition as granite: quartz, feldspar and mica, arranged in layers. It occurs in the same widely varied color range as granite, including: gray, green, pink, red and brown, and occasionally white and black.

Gneisses vary according to the rocks from which they originated, some being sedimentary, others igneous, and are usually named according to the chief mineral in them. Thus, there is hornblende gneiss, syenite gneiss, etc. Gneiss by itself usually means mica gneiss, but the term has become so generalized that it is commonly applied to any crystalline rock with mineral veins.

Location — Gneisses are scattered throughout the world. Good examples occur in mountainous areas in Germany, Scotland and Scandinavia. In the United States — in the Rockies and Appalachians.

Use — Ideal for building purposes.

SOAPSTONE: *Chemical Formula* $(H_2Mg_3(SiO_3)_4)$ — consists mainly of talc and consequently is very soft. It also contains other minerals, such as quartz, chlorite and magnetite. *Color* — dark gray or green; *cleavage* — none; *luster* — greasy; *special characteristics* — Soapstone is found in huge sheets which may be several hundred feet thick and several thousand feet long. It is soft in texture and can, therefore, be cut into varied sizes and shapes. It has a distinctively soapy touch, a characteristic which is highlighted in its name.

Fascinating Facts — It has an ancient history of usage since cooking utensils of primitive peoples have been unearthed made of soapstone. It was also shaped by the early Indians into decorative pieces.

Location — The United States produces more than 50 per cent of the soapstone used annually. Virginia is one of the major soapstone areas. Other states where it is found include: New York, Vermont, California, North Carolina, Pennsylvania, Rhode Island, and Massachusetts.

Use — Noted for its ability to withstand acid deterioration, soapstone is found highly practical for laboratory work tables. In addition, its remarkable powers of heat retention make it ideal for insulation. A large percentage is ground up into powder where it forms a base for such diverse products as paint, roofing, and cosmetic powder.

SLATE: *Chemical Formula* — produced from clay and shale which have been constricted and deformed by the weight of the earth. Commonest minerals in shale are quartz, mica, chlorite and carbonaceous material. *Color* — gray or black. A high percentage of chlorite may turn it green; iron oxides will color it yellow, red and brown; *cleavage* — splits into thin layers, known as slaty cleavage. This is a unique type of splitting. It does not occur parallel to the original bedding, instead it proceeds at erratic angles, according to the shifting and slipping that occurred when the bed was caught in the midst of mountain re-adjustments.

Location — Wales is the leading country for the production of slate. In the United States there are slate quarries at New York, Vermont, Pennsylvania, Maine and Maryland.

Use — Known for its resistance to weather and fire, slate is extensively used in the roofing field. Also adapts well for blackboards and laboratory tables.

MARBLE: *Chemical Formula* — Marble is metamorphosed limestone. All marble contains crystals of the minerals calcite or dolomite, which in their pure state are white, and this is considered the best grade of marble. *Color* — May be gray, black, yellow, pink or red. The color may be even throughout but usually is mottled or "marbled"; *hardness* — 3.

Fascinating Facts — The Romans and Greeks used marble extensively in architecture, and it still is high in popularity for modern sculpture, monuments and imposing edifices. Architects and artists make fine distinctions in the various types of marbles, according to color and outward appearance:

STATUARY MARBLES: These are pure white in color, massive in size.

ORNAMENTAL MARBLES: This group, in contrast, are valued for their bright colors.

ARCHITECTURAL MARBLES: These marbles have uniform texture and color and the extra advantage of being able to be cut into comparatively thin slabs or blocks. This renders them desirable for columns, walls, and floors. Marbles are also used for steps.

Location — Carrara, Italy is world-renowned for its marble quarries, which have been worked for 2,000 years. In the United States, the leading marble state is Vermont, followed closely by Massachusetts, Tennessee, Pennsylvania, Alabama, Georgia, New York and Colorado.

JADE: *Chemical Formula* — Jade commonly refers to two different metamorphic rocks: jadeite or nephrite. Some geologists prefer to classify both varieties as minerals.

NEPHRITE: This is the common source of jade; it is regarded as the true jade. *Color* — dark green, white, yellow, gray, red and black; the most precious type is a dark green jade, called Chinese jade; *luster* — waxy; *hardness* — 6; *specific gravity* — 3.

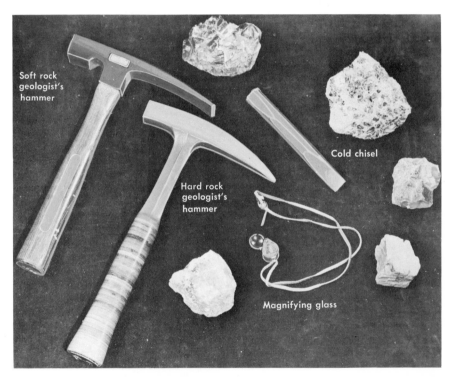

Soft rock geologist's hammer

Hard rock geologist's hammer

Cold chisel

Magnifying glass

Equipment for rock hunting

Fascinating Facts — The Chinese are known for the intricacy and beauty of their jade carvings.

Location — Today nephrite comes largely from New Zealand. In the United States, nephrite deposits have been found in Alaska and Wyoming.

JADEITE is lighter-colored, somewhat harder and heavier (*specific gravity* — 3.2 - 3.4) than nephrite. It is a much rarer mineral and is found chiefly in Burma, Japan and Mexico.

EQUIPMENT FOR ROCK HOUNDS ON ROCK HUNTS

Here is the basic equipment you will need when planning a rock collecting expedition:

1 — Pocket knife.

2 — Sturdy hammer. You may want to treat yourself to a geologist's hammer which comes with a special head. One type is flat at one end and has a sharply pointed pick at the opposite end, to aid in splitting or prying rocks loose. Another type, sometimes called a soft rock hammer, has a flat head on one end and a broad tapered pick at the other end.

3 — Cold chisel for chipping fragments of rock from larger ones. Two sizes are recommended: one measuring one-half inch or slightly more; and a second one which is an inch wide.

4 — Steel rule or tape measure. A 6-foot rule is adequate for measuring outcroppings from which samples are taken.

5 — Magnifying glass. One with two or three lenses will serve your purpose.

6 — Paper or cloth sacks for samples of soft materials, such as soil, gravel, clay, volcanic ash, etc. Small, discarded, thoroughly cleaned medicine bottles also make safe carrying containers for sandy substances.

7 — Newspapers to wrap around each sample.

8 — A canvas knapsack to carry the rocks home.

9 — A notebook to record data, which brings us to the next important subject which has to do with:

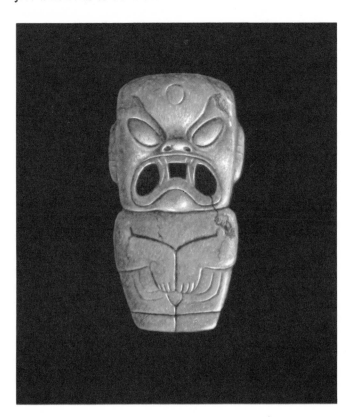

JADE

42

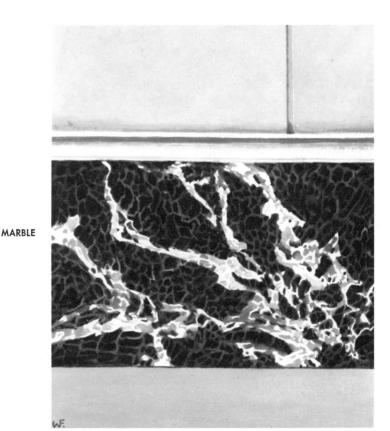

MARBLE

RECORD KEEPING FOR YOUR ROCK COLLECTION

Keeping notes on your rock specimens begins with the first rock you gather which you seriously plan to include in your collection. A few brief notes should be jotted down, giving such essentials as: the date found, location, and general description. The rock should also be assigned a number. This will help you when adding further facts, upon your return home, and for organizing and keeping track of your collection as it expands.

There is an easy method of labeling used by professional rock hounds which you will find invaluable. Using India ink, write a series of numbers, beginning with No. 1, on a strip of adhesive tape. Scissor the strips apart, and stick on a piece of wax paper, where it will be easy to lift them off for immediate use. As soon as you find the first rock specimen that you are going to keep, put the adhesive label with the lowest number on it, and then write this identifying number with the accompanying data in your notebook.

The adhesive tape is only a temporary method of labeling. As your collection grows, you will want to set up a more permanent system. The kind of labeling you ultimately use will depend on where you store your specimens.

STORAGE

At the beginning, you may use egg cartons, jewelry boxes or cigar and shirt boxes, which have been partitioned off with cardboard or strips of plywood. You may also display your specimens on book shelves.

PERMANENT STORAGE: As you accumulate a large collection, you may want to buy tiers of drawers from supply houses, or you can make a basic cabinet or chest with interchangeable drawers, made of a plywood bottom and plain wood sides.

The advanced rock hound stores his specimens in individual cardboard trays, which helps to keep them in order and prevent damage. These may be purchased from supply houses or else they can be made of cardboard and gummed tape.

Since the rocks vary in size, the trays should be made in various sizes; for example, you might have two small trays take up the same area as a large one.

For exhibition purposes, you may consider the idea of securing the rock to the bottom of the drawer with thin wire. The descriptive label would then go below the sample.

Storage tray for a rock collection

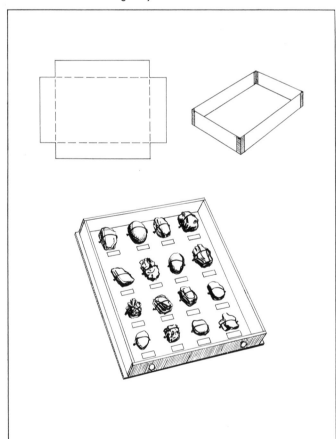

In other cases, where a box is used, the label may be placed under the specimen or on the inside cover of the box; where a shelf is used, the label can be fastened on just below the specimen.

For permanent reference, a dot of white enamel should be painted on a clear, clean area on the rock. After the enamel has dried, paint on the number with black enamel, using a fine-tipped brush.

Your label need only give basic details, such as:

Granite (name of rock)

(identifying number) No. 1   Igneous (kind of rock)

Barre, Vermont (location)

Many collectors prefer a looseleaf notebook since they can add or delete pages. Information may also be put on 3x5 index cards.

Rocks are a part of the earth itself. Starting a rock collection is like gathering a treasure house of precious bits of hard knowledge about the world you live in — and the world that has been.

Storage cabinet for a rock collection

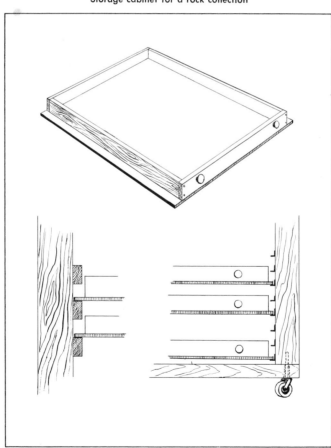

TURQUOISE

THE SCIENCE-HOBBY SERIES

A Check-list of the Most Common Minerals, Rocks and Metals Found in the Fifty States:

Nebraska: limestone, clay, pumicite, agate.

Nevada: cinnabar, copper, galena, gold, halite, limestone, obsidian, silver, slate, sulphur.

New Hampshire: beryl, fluorite, galena, garnet, granite, graphite, mica, quartz, rutile, soapstone, tourmaline.

New Jersey: apatite, calcite, copper, corundum, dolomite, fluorite, magnetite, milky quartz, pyrite, zinc, tourmaline.

New Mexico: aragonite, azurite, amethyst, barite, calcite, gold, halite, limestone, malachite, shale, silver, turquoise.

New York: apatite, basalt, calcite, feldspar, galena, garnet, graphite, dolomite, halite, mica, quartz, limestone, pyrite, talc, tourmaline, zircon, barite, gypsum, magnetite.

North Carolina: beryl, iron, emerald, garnet, magnetite, mica, orthoclase, salt, talc, rutile.

North Dakota: lignite.

Ohio: alum, calcite, fluorite, gypsum, halite, sulphur.

Oklahoma: barite, calcite, dolomite, galena, marcasite, sphalerite, sulphur, gypsum.

Oregon: azurite, cinnabar, gold, pyrite, malachite, chromite.

Pennsylvania: asbestos, beryl, copper, corundum, galena, graphite, limestone, magnetite, mica, nickel, smoky quartz, talc, yellow and white tourmaline, zircon, coal.

Rhode Island: amethyst, feldspar, graphite, manganese, magnetite, talc, granite.

South Carolina: gold, magnetite, rutile, tourmaline, zircon, kaolin.

South Dakota: beryl, feldspar, gold, gypsum, mica, rose quartz, tin, uraninite, bentonite, wolframite.

Tennessee: alum, apatite, fluorite, gypsum, pyrite, zinc, marble.

Texas: calcite, cinnabar, halite, limestone, sulphur, gypsum.

Utah: galena, halite, limestone, pyrite, sandstone, silver, gold, copper, topaz, uranium.

Vermont: asbestos, feldspar, garnet, marble, pyrite, quartz, tourmaline, slate, granite, talc.

Virginia: gold, pyrite, quartz, rutile, stalactites and stalagmites, zinc, coal, soapstone.

Washington: gold, quartz, copper, magnesite, tourmaline.

West Virginia: hematite, limestone, coal.

Wisconsin: barite, calcite, galena, pyrite, zinc, hematite.

Wyoming: amethyst, asbestos, calcite, quartz, sulphur, phosphate.

We specialize in publishing quality books for
young people. For a complete list please write

LERNER PUBLICATIONS COMPANY

241 First Avenue North, Minneapolis, Minnesota 55401